2019
GRAND PRIX
GUIDE

SNIFF PETROL

2019 Grand Prix Guide by Sniff Petrol

ISBN: 9781799124993

Published by Sniff Petrol Limited
sniffpetrol.com

CONTENTS

FOREWORD
BY TED KRAVITZ

Sorry. I'm here now.

F1 DATES FOR YOUR DIARY

15 March 2019 – Stroll makes first embarrassing error.

5 April 2019 – Ferrari start talking a little too confidently about their championship hopes.

14 April 2019 – First major movie star inexplicably appears in paddock in place you'd not expect them to be.

11 May 2019 – Moment when it seems things really couldn't get any worse for Williams.

12 May 2019 – Moment when things somehow get even worse for Williams.

28 June 2019 - First rumour that Daniil Kvyat is going to get booted out of Toro Rosso mid-season.

23 July 2019 – Kimi Raikkonen starting to think this team isn't Ferrari.

5 August 2019 – Remember to mute all drivers on Instagram unless you like pictures taken by people having nicer holidays than you.

1 September 2019 – Ferrari adopt optimistic 'it's not over yet' tone.

2 September 2019 - Ferrari enter slough of despair.

2 December 2019 – Kimi Raikkonen realises he has left Ferrari.

RACE 1: AUSTRALIA

Date: 17 March
Location: Melbourne
Full name: The Tim Tam Alf Stewart Hoon-o-drome
Circuit type: Ripper

The action starts in Melbourne (known locally as 'Melbo') where the home crowd ('crowdo') will be hoping for a strong performance from Aussie driver Daniel Ricciardo ('Danno') who has replaced departed hero Mark Webber ('Webbo') in their affections. Ricciardo ('Ricciardo-o') will have his work cut out on the flowing streets of the city, especially as this year the mayor has forgotten to apply for the permit that closes the roads to other traffic. We can therefore expect a strong showing from utes and some kind of Toyota that isn't sold in Europe.

FIVE FACTS ABOUT AUSTRALIA

1. The expression 'no worries' comes from early 20th century Prime Minister Norman Worringtons.
2. Of the 10 most poisonous animals in the world, 13 live in Australia. Two others are thinking of moving there.
3. The deadliest spider in Australia is the blue gollawolla which has a bite equivalent to 19 cans of strong lager.
4. The most dangerous snake is the brown and red Australian hoolygoolywong which gets into your house through the attic and then just lies around on your sofa eating your snacks and talking about this band it's in.
5. Many people say that the national anthem of Australia is *Down Under* by Men At Work but that's just an Aussie joke. The national anthem is *You're The Voice* by John Farnham.

THE TEAMS: MERCEDES

LEWIS HAMILTON
Nationality: British
Accent nationality: Not sure.
Seems to hover somewhere over Novia Scotia.
Number: 44
Championship position last year: 1st
Nickname: The Hammer

VALTTERI BOTTAS
Nationality: Finnish
Number: 77
Championship position last year: 5th
Nickname: The Reasonable Situation

THE TEAMS: MERCEDES

Full name: Mercedes-AMG Petronas #blessed
Motorsport
Car: F1 W10 EQ Power+
Engine: Mercedes
Championship position last year: 1st

The reigning champions arrive in 2019 hoping to secure their sixth constructors' title in a row while giving Lewis Hamilton his sixth drivers' title. Oh, and maybe let the other guy do some stuff. He never asks, but they can tell he'd really like to win another race or something, especially as he didn't win a single one last year. Not that he's one to complain, preferring instead to hang around happily helping out however he can, like an obedient robot man-baby. Mercedes have to be favourites to win everything again this year, despite their pre-season protestations about how much work they have to do and how good Ferrari were in testing, which the drivers and team solemnly delivered while standing in front of a massive pile of sandbags. Probably.

GET THE LOOK – LEWIS HAMILTON

Most F1 drivers dress like an American IT specialist getting ready for a corporate away weekend in Palm Springs but not Lewis Hamilton. The British driver is famed for his 'fashion forward' style outside of work and it's a look you might be tempted to copy. But beware. Dressing like Lewis Hamilton isn't as simple as travelling back to Milwaukee in 1994 and mugging a teenager for his clothes, even though it looks like it is. With careful preparation, however, you too could have the Lewis Hamilton look. Here are some good ways to start;

- Rummage through Jackie Stewart's bins until you find some old trousers to wear as a snood.
- Steal an old man's hat.
- Take some acid and then go on a credit card bender in Millets.
- Go onto the ladies' section of the ASOS website and just start madly clicking on things with your eyes shut.
- Cover yourself in glue and then roll around in the stock room of a charity shop.
- Steal the lost property bin from a Latvian municipal swimming pool.
- Have your head shrunk so all your existing hats look weird.
- Engage in a wager to win a taxi driver's clothes.
- Keep your existing clothes but attack them with scissors and then put them on upside down.

RACE 2: BAHRAIN

Date: 31 March
Location: Sakhir
Full name: Bahrain International Circuit Of Everything
Is Absolutely Nice And Not Being Tortured Here
Circuit type: Dusty

The first of those races that make Kimi Raikkonen a bit
panicky, Bahrain is sure to live up to its reputation as a
barely notable event that happens because some old men
did a deal for an enormous amount of money and it's
contractually pretty watertight so tough titties. The Sakhir
circuit is a high speed track and that means it's sure to be
tough on engines, brakes and any part of the car that is
openly gay which will be taken to a local prison and
tortured without trial.

FIVE FACTS ABOUT BAHRAIN

1. The name Bahrain derives from two words, 'ba'
   meaning 'beat' and 'hrain' meaning 'your wife,
   without fear of penalty'.
2. Bahrain is built on an archipelago of over 30 islands,
   each one slightly less interesting than the last.
3. Animals found in Bahrain include deer, rabbit and an
   elephant, although that's just on holiday there and
   normally lives in Chichester.
4. Every year Bahrain holds a special 'day of oil' in
   which everyone is encouraged to say thank fuck for all
   this oil otherwise we'd be really screwed.
5. The most famous Bahraini celebrity is Abbas Khalifi,
   more commonly known by his stage name, 'Man Of
   Several Briefcases'.

THE RULE CHANGES

There are various rule changes for 2019, most aimed at reducing the amount of turbulent, 'dirty' air dumped immediately behind the car. This mucky air is unhelpful to the car behind, compromising their aerodynamics and denying them the chance to overtake unless they're Max Verstappen and they just go for it anyway. Off-mic F1 technical director Ross Brawn and a team including Fozzie-voiced ex-Williamsist Pat Symonds have worked on a fix for this with the following changes;

Front wing – 200mm wider, 20mm higher, moved forward by 25mm, and of simplified design, so it can still look like a weird razor marketed as the Turbothrust Power Slide Five but can't appear to have been smeared in glue and driven into a pile of carbon fibre shelf brackets.
Rear wing – 100mm wider, 20mm higher, nicer smell.
DRS – Opening extended by 20mm
DFS – Sale extended until June
Bargeboards – 150mm lower and 100mm further forward, although you can still catch your foot on them when you get in.
Brake ducts – Simplified. These had become a manager of air around the front wheels. Now they will only be a deputy manager, and they don't work Tuesdays unless Mrs Millington is off sick again.

These are all small changes but when added together the difference they make could be pretty much fuck all, at least going by the reaction from drivers after testing. Oh well.

Other changes for 2019 include;

Fuel – full load now permitted to be 110 kilos rather than 105. You can get a sense of what this is like by going to your local Esso garage and asking for an extra five kilos of petrol, please.

Lights – Two extra high-mounted lights on the rear wing to be used when on wet or intermediate tyres. This is to improve safety in bad weather, and also because they look cool.

Weight – The weight of the driver is now taken into account separately. This is to avoid penalising heavier drivers, although don't expect any of the current field to start troughing down on pies. Not unless Juan Pablo Montoya makes an unexpected comeback.

Biometric gloves – The driver's gloves now measure his pulse and blood oxygen levels and transmit that data back to the medical centre in a system described by scientists as "that be some futuristic shit right there".

Helmet – For 2019 every helmet is stronger, so it can better withstand impacts and also the pressure of having a ridiculously intricate and needlessly busy design painted all over it that somehow manages to be unique and yet completely unmemorable.

Chequered flag - The official finish is now a chequered light while the waved flag is just for ceremony. This is to prevent some idiot from accidentally telling one of Little Mix or someone you've never heard of from a Lithuanian soup commercial to wave it a lap early.

TYRES

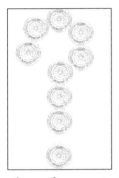

Pirelli has come up with a new system to simplify the tyre choices for 2019. Gone is last year's 'rainbow' line-up of seven confusing options, and in comes a new, more straightforward system in which teams have a choice at any given race of just three tyres; soft, medium, hard, wet and intermediate. This means there will be no more supersoft or ultrasoft, except of course when there is.

Pirelli's simplified three tyre system is based around there being just five tyres, plus another two. Behind the scenes these are labelled with new codes from C1 to C5, but for each race two of those don't exist, apart from C3. As you would expect, C1 is the hardest and C5 isn't. All the fans need to know is that every race weekend the teams will get to pick from just three colours which are red, yellow and white corresponding to hardness in the reverse order.

What's interesting is that, because the three tyres are actually five, for any given weekend a red could be a C4 or C5 while a yellow could also be a C4 and a white could be a C2 unless that is also a yellow on a different weekend, and one in which the yellow isn't a C3 because that is red.

As you can see, a much simplerer system than before. Unless you're colour blind or not concentrating.

RACE 3: CHINA

Date: 14 April
Location: Shanghai
Full name: The People's Circuit of Unoccupied Seating
Circuit type: Meh

This year's Chinese race is the 1000th Grand Prix in F1 history, an honour that organisers hope will distract from the usual unremarkableness of the event at that track with the big things over the pit straight. No, not that one, the other one. It's hard to believe there have been one thousand Formula 1 races and that Michael Douglas has been at several of them. China's F1 fans are of course delighted at this landmark, or at least one of them is. The other one said he wasn't particularly bothered.

FIVE FACTS ABOUT CHINA

1. Over the past 30 years China has slowly shifted to a more relaxed form of communism where you can't overthrow the government but you can have an iPhone so shut up.
2. By government decree, the weather across all of China must be a bit muggy.
3. Even minor crimes in China can be punishable by up to five years in a cage making unbranded Android handsets.
4. On average, a new skyscraper is completed in China every two days. As a result there are now more skyscrapers in the country than there are businesses that need offices.
5. The most popular job in China is skyscraper builder. The second is window cleaner. The third is Thierry Boutsen impersonator.

THE TEAMS: FERRARI

SEBASTIAN VETTEL
Nationality: German
Number: 5
Championship position last year: 2nd
Nickname: The Big Huff

CHARLES LECLERC
Nationality: Not French.
You think he's French but he's not. He's a Monopod.
Number: 16
Championship position last year: 13th
Nickname: It Is Him, Leclerc

THE TEAMS: FERRARI

Full name: Scuderia Ferrari Mission Winnow Mmm Lovely Relaxing Smokes
Car: SF90
Engine: Ferrari
Championship position last year: 2nd

Ferrari looked promising at the start of last year, as they often do, and long-time fans were on the edge of their seats as they waited to see how the team would completely fuck it up. It took a while, but then sure enough they made some silly mistakes and Sebastian Vettel got all flustered and angry and then they pissed away the title in the almost-but-not-quite style that has marked the last decade. In Ferrari's defence, the method they used to ultimately disappoint was a lot more complicated than in some seasons but the team nevertheless reacted in their traditional manner, which was to have a hissy fit and sack the man in charge. The departure of swarthy team boss Maurizio Arrivabene might come as a relief since he looked like he made the motorhomes smell of fags and went through the drivers' stuff when were out in the cars. Arrivabene has been replaced by Mattia Binotto who will be hoping his tenure at the team is more Todt and less Mattiacci. There's a change in the car too as Sebastian Vettel, who increasingly resembles a peevish old lady complaining about inadequate provision of napkins at the church hall jam sale, is joined by promising youngster Charles Leclerc, replacing one-man disinterest typhoon Kimi Raikkonen who moves to Alfa Romeo, although he probably wasn't paying attention and will continue to show up at the Ferrari factory for a bit.

FAMOUS QUOTES FROM F1 HISTORY

"I came here this weekend to do two things; win a race and have sexual intercourse. And I've already had sexual intercourse three times this morning, plus a wank."

JAMES HUNT (1976)

RACE 4: AZERBAIJAN

Date: 28 April
Location: Baku
Full name: The National Circuit of Many Widths
Circuit type: Downtown

Formula 1 returns to Azerbaijan which is an ongoing nightmare for the organisers who thought F1 worked like the Eurovision Song Contest and they wouldn't have to host it more than once as long as they didn't win. As a result of a misread contract, racing is back on a track that is fast and slow, narrow and wide, old and new, in Europe and not anywhere fucking near Europe, why did they used to pretend it was? As part of a PR campaign, anyone attending this year's race is entered into a draw to win a local prize, such as the chance to arrest someone for no reason and then beat them repeatedly in a cell.

FIVE FACTS ABOUT AZERBAIJAN

1. The Azerbaijanian government is thinking about removing the I in the country's name. "It's just so pointless," said a spokeispersion.
2. The national animal of Azerbaijan is a horse.
3. Because of the above, most of the national anthem is the word 'horse' shouted at increasingly loud volume until the horse turns up and asks them to keep it down because it's late and she's got a meeting tomorrow.
4. The tourist trade in Baku struggled for many years until it was realised that, due to a translation error, overseas promotional materials accidentally billed it as "the city where you will get kicked in the back".
5. Azerbaijan's top-rated TV show is called Thierry Boutsen's World Of Decking, now into its 18th series.

WHAT IS MISSION WINNOW?

Many F1 fans have been confused by the mysterious branding on the Ferraris and have been asking, what is this Mission Winnow business all about?

Marketing manager NICOLA O'TINE explains all.

Nothing seems to spark up some cool, delicious controversy in Formula 1 like a new sponsor, especially one that isn't well known. Indeed, some F1 fans seemed determined to smoke out the truth about Mission Winnow and its appearance on two machines amongst the 20 pack of cars on the grid.

Let me start by slowly blowing out some of the myths about the great feeling of Mission Winnow and putting a healthy filter on some of the rumours. This is a brand that draws deeply on heritage, but it's also about lighting up a way into the future.

Mission Winnow is not about the drag of selling products in the old-fashioned way or giving you a load of delicious puff that is a fag to consume; it is about gently taking in the great feeling of the future. Let me give you a smooth, mild taste of what I mean.

For years we have kept tabs on what Formula 1 fans like, even if sometimes our efforts to tell fans about exciting new things were stubbed out. Today, we want to step outside the conventional for five minutes or so and take in some of the fresh, delicious taste of a new paradigm.

That's why Mission Winnow is a state of mind, as well as a deep breath of something hot but new. As we say today, it's lit. To really understand Mission Winnow, however, you have to take it firmly between your fingers and allow yourself to suck in its qualities.

That's because, above all, Mission Winnow just wants you to relax, whether after a big dinner or first thing in the morning with a coffee and then a dump. Wherever you step out onto the balcony to do it, we know you'll get a rush from drawing firmly on what Mission Winnow has to share.

I hope that gives you a smooth, Virginia flavour of where you can find us in all good newsagents.

POINTS

There's a change to the scoring system for 2019 as the driver who sets the fastest lap during each race will receive an extra championship point, as long as they finish in the top 10.

Here are some other points system revisions F1 bosses are said to be considering;

- 1 extra point for any driver who can go a whole race weekend without starting a sentence with 'for sure'.

- 2 extra points for any driver who can go a whole race weekend without saying that 'the guys' did a 'good job'.

- 1 extra point for the fastest walk through the paddock alongside a person in team-branded kit while a camera tries to track in front of you.

- 5 extra points if you do your last lap entirely sideways, like a drift king in an S13 Silvia.

- 10 extra points for any driver who makes the Spanish Grand Prix more interesting.

RACE 5: SPAIN

Date: 12 May
Location: Barcelona
Full circuit name: El Circuito del Boredom Masivo
Circuit type: Tedious

Like that one really boring person who always turns up at parties and ruins the atmosphere, Spain remains on the F1 calendar despite promising no excitement whatsoever. A popular track with drivers, but only because they've been here in testing so it's easier to remember, the Barcelona track is also popular with anyone who's already got plans that Sunday and won't feel a pang of regret about going out rather than slumping in front of the TV watching a life-sapping procession that has the commentators rambling aimlessly off-topic like embarrassed radio DJs by about lap 17.

FIVE FACTS ABOUT SPAIN

1. The main languages of Spain are Spanish, Catalan, and English spoken loudly with an Essex accent.
2. The controversial sport of bullfighting is in decline in Spain because young people are more interested in torturing animals with their smartphones.
3. The Spanish want Gibraltar because they really need to increase the national stock of poisonous monkeys and retired London taxi drivers.
4. The Spanish national anthem is unusual in that it has no words. That's why at the bottom of the Spanish flag it says 'ask about our lyrics competition'.
5. Spain is actually made up of 17 smaller areas. It should have been six but the government thought they all sounded delicious and over-ordered.

THE TEAMS: RED BULL

MAX VERSTAPPEN
Nationality: Dutch
Number: 33
Championship position last year: 4th
Nickname: Maximum Verstappening

PIERRE GASLY
Nationality: French
Number: 10
Championship position last year: 15th
Nickname: Peter Ghastly

THE TEAMS: RED BULL

Full name: Aston Martin Red Bull Marketing
Car: RB15
Engine: Honda
Championship position last year: 3rd

There are changes afoot for the team that used to win everything although that's starting to feel like a long time ago now. First of all, they've lost the services of perma-cheery Daniel Ricciardo and will pair insolent youth Max Verstappen and his but-that's-the-bit-of-track-I-wanted-to-drive-on attitude with promising Toro Rosso refugee Pierre Gasly who can look quick, though not as much as he can look like the annoying jock character from a nineties American high school movie. Red Bull's engine supplier changes for 2019 too as they're finally able to stop pretending those shitty factory seconds from Renault were made by a watch company and can concentrate on pretending that other parts of the car are made by Aston Martin. Their new Honda power units are showing some potential, and they're sure to become stronger as the season gets underway, especially if they can find some way to harness the anguished screams coming out of the McLaren pit. Overall, the RB15 could be a strong contender this season, even if design maestro and flesh-covered super computer Adrian Newey seems permanently distracted designing road cars and boats and generally carrying on like someone who wants to end a relationship but is too embarrassed to just come out and say something.

FAMOUS QUOTES FROM F1 HISTORY

"I don't want to point the finger, but it's plainly obvious this is everybody else's fault."

NIGEL MANSELL (1986)

RACE 6: MONACO

Date: 26 May
Location: Monte Carlo
Full circuit name: Circuit de Taxrelief
Circuit type: Squashed

Monaco remains a crass exercise in gaudy wealth and artlessly contrived glamour against a backdrop of minimal overtaking and moneyed disinterest and, as such, is the very bedrock of F1. Drivers like it because if they bin it into the barrier at Mirabeau they can probably walk home, and fans like it because they'll get loads of anecdote mileage out of the time they stayed too late on Saturday and had to pay €600 for a 25 minute cab ride back to Nice. Monaco is rarely a classic race, but it's a great reminder that nothing attracts absolute twats like a yacht.

FIVE FACTS ABOUT MONACO

1. Geologists estimate that Monaco may eventually crumble into the sea from the ever-increasing weight of buildings, jewellery and high-end Russian hookers.
2. The loudest sound ever heard on earth was the words "JESUS CHRIST" uttered by a man from Tunbridge Wells upon seeing the bill for three beers in Casino Square on the Friday before a Monaco Grand Prix.
3. Many F1 drivers live in Monaco, including Thierry Boutsen who has one of the principality's largest areas of decking.
4. It's not illegal to appear to be enjoying yourself in Monaco, that's just the way the Princess looks.
5. The correct name for someone from Monaco is 'a Monocle'.

AN INTRODUCTION TO F1

New to Formula 1? Don't worry, American reporter KENNY SPORTLEMAN is here to explain the basics

Hey sports fans. Kenny Sportleman here for KYWXZ drivetime sports, coming hard in your car across the quad county area. So here's a little something new for you, and it's an awesome European-style auto racing series called Formulation One.

Some of you folks may be unfamiliar with this up-and-coming new vehicle sport that's taking the world by storm so let's take a moment to hear more about why this series is one to watch for the future.

Formullered One takes place over 21 games, sometimes called Grand Pricks, and these occur all across the world, in places as exotic as England, Italy, Australasia, China and Great Britain from March thru December. Each race battle occurs across a series of days beginning with some unregulated practise throws on Friday, leading to the solo racing speed trials upon Saturday. These occur across three quarters, the first of which involves all 20 players engaged in a sprint-style sudden death match against the countdown clock. At the end of this stretch, the five weakest contenders are eliminated and the action re-sets for a second individual speed demonstration, after which just 10 men are left for a final single shot speed test, out of which the fastest player will emerge and take first base on the line-out for the following day's head-to-head race-style event. This is the main attraction in Frimula One and sees all 20 driving stars, each paired into a team of two, going against each other in a multi-player battle royale. It's 90 minutes of incredible vehicle sport action, punctuated only by the mandatory tire rotation time-outs of which there must be at least one. These enforced sports breaks can be used tactically to gain field advantage over rivals, without which players must engage in an overtaking offensive in order to gain greater access to the score zone which exists only for the final 10 combatants, ensuring that play remains intense right up until the checking flag that signals game over. I've witnessed Form Of The One for myself and let me tell you folks, it certainly passes the Sportleman Scrimmage test!

So who are the main players in this so-called Gran Pree series? Well, the MVP is a guy called Louis Hamiltown, coming out of Steven Age, England, and a five time champion for both the Brackley Bears and, previously, the Woking Wombats. Hammertime scored the world series title last year and yestertimes before that in 2017, though his 2016 season was not to be as the driving excellence pendant was lifted by team association Nicko Rozberg, now retired from the sport because he could not be assed. Roastberger's replacement is one Valerie Boatass out of Finnerland and this guy appears to pose no threat to Hamington and his ambitions to lift a sixth trophy bowl to signal supreme victory in this sport we sometimes call Effone. A greater magnitude of challenge comes from Sebasterone Vettelle of Germany, Europe who already holds a quadlude of titles and hopes to secure more with the backing of his team, the Maranello Marvels, who oftentimes show great form only to lack the fortitude to carry it to the win zone. Vethell himself may also come under pressure from within his own pack as new signing Chuck Leclerk is sure to be on the offensive in the opening sectors of the season. Long time Formoola Wan watchers also state that fresh challenge could come from former World Series champions the Milton Keynes Meerkats, and in particular their front backer Mack Verstapperen who is known for his aggressive passing play to achieve maximum position on the point ladder. But as they always say in F-One, there are extra yards in experience and that's why this reporter will keep a keen eye on Kim E. Raykenon, freshly transferred to the Swiss Stallions who have themselves recently re-located from Sawber to the great city of Alpha Romeo, in what promises to be an awesome season of non-oval auto events.

If you're interested in seeing more of Formulaone, the great news is that the sports series comes to the US in November with a regulation showcase event down there in Austin, Texas. Get yourself along, you won't be very disappointed. And hey, if you're in the city, try McNabbabbies for the ribs. Tell Lurlan that Kenny sent you, she'll fix you up with some extra hot chacha and a side of real meat cruffins.

For KYWXZ drivetime, I'm Kenny Sportleman, just as excited as you should be for the new series of Formulation Number One!

RACE 7: CANADA

Date: 9 June
Location: Montreal
Full name: Circuit Gilles Villeneuve et Aussi Son Fils
Irritant, Jacques
Circuit type: Walled

Everybody likes the Canadian Grand Prix because it's in Canada and run by Canadians and how could you not enjoy that? It's like having a race inside Michael Bublé. Montreal is a short, snappy track with plenty of challenges including the infamous Wall of Champions which can catch out the most talented drivers and Lance Stroll. Speaking of which, the crowd will be rooting for the local boy because they're Canadian and therefore too nice to say he's just a ridiculous rich kid playing at brumm brumms.

FIVE FACTS ABOUT CANADA

1. Canada recently legalised recreational marijuana after deciding that a stack of pancakes and maple syrup for breakfast wasn't making everyone sluggish enough.
2. Canada is famed for its weary tolerance towards the United States, like a pleasant family that's nice to some inbred, gun-toting simpletons next door because they might need them to watch the house while they're out of town.
3. Canada is the second largest country in the world but doesn't like to boast about it.
4. It also has over half of the world's lakes, but is always trying to give them away so it doesn't look greedy.
5. Famous Canadians include every single Hollywood actor, comedian and musician you thought was from the US.

THE TEAMS: RENAULT

DANIEL RICCIARDO
Nationality: Australian
Number: 3
Championship position last year: 6th
Nickname: Cream of Badger

NICO HULKENBERG
Nationality: German
Number: 27
Championship position last year: 7th
Nickname: The Hulkenberg

THE TEAMS: RENAULT

Full name: Renault F1 Team should we include 'sport' here? No? Oh, okay. I thought we used to. Shit, is the machine still on?
Car: R.S.19
Engine: Renault
Championship position last year: 4th

The team based in the beautiful French village of Enstone in Oxfordshire has improved steadily ever since they got rid of Jolyon Palmer to the extent that last year they confidently grabbed fourth place in the constructors' standings, making them official kings of the midfield. They'll be looking to build on that in 2019, while realistically probably coming fourth again, and their quest will be made easier by an excellent driver line-up that pairs the safe hands of hardy perennial Nico Hulkenberg with the cheery demeanour of human grinning machine Daniel Ricciardo, a man who brakes so late he sometimes finishes the race, goes home and is busy rooting around in the fridge looking for a snack when he suddenly goes, "Ohhhhhh" and twitches his foot. All told, things look positive for Renault in 2019 and their only problem could be the requirement to use engines made by Renault.

LOOK AHEAD TO MIAMI

Plans for a Miami Grand Prix in 2019 couldn't be agreed in time but Formula 1 bosses are determined that for 2020 racing will come to the city where, according to Will Smith, you can 'bounce' in a club 'where the heat is on'. Seems a bit wasteful, given how warm it is outside. If anything, it's going to make the place so suffocatingly hot it'll be impossible to enjoy yourself.

Here are some of the contractual issues currently being ironed out ahead of next year's planned event;

- Can't call circuit 'The Douche-o-drome'.

- Can't replace normal pace car with white Testarossa.

- Unsafe to have all drivers dressed entirely in linen.

- Race security cannot be entrusted to 'Eddy's cousin'.

- Podium ceremony cannot ditch champagne and invite drivers to celebrate by tearing open a huge bag of cocaine.

RACE 8: FRANCE

Date: 23 June
Location: Le Castellet
Full name: Circuit D'Une Petite Boisson Qui Ressemble Spunk
Circuit type: Stripy

The event known locally as 'The French Big Prize' returned in 2018 after a 10 year break, and immediately became known for its world class traffic problems. The organisers have promised to tackle the issue this year by asking a further two gendarmes to stand by the side of the road looking disdainful as they listlessly wave a baton. For 2019 the pit lane entry will be moved, although not without a lot of huffing first. Overall, the re-born Paul Ricard circuit is already a firm favourite amongst fans of enormous run-off areas.

FIVE FACTS ABOUT FRANCE

1. One of the most popular pastimes in France is not giving a shit what you think.
2. The French have a special word for fizzy white wine.
3. Due to an obscure by-law, all French villages must close down at 7:55pm and everyone must just go to bed or keep really, really quiet, and this applies even to the three surly teenagers who spent the afternoon monopolising the babyfoot table in the café.
4. Even France realises the importance of health & safety which is why people now wear high visibility jackets before tipping over cars and setting them on fire.
5. France's most popular racing driver is Thierry Boutsen, even though he keeps trying to tell them he's Belgian.

DON'T GET ME STARTED ON ROMAIN GROSJEAN

BY GUENTHER STEINER

Oh my God, don't get me started on that asshole Romain Grosjean. That kid, he is a pain in my asshole all of the time. Don't ask me again, he is like the fucking tits on a fish. Jesus Christ, okay, listen, I'll explain this to you.

Like, we have to put stickers on all the glass doors in the factory so he doesn't walk into them and break his stupid fucking face, right. And I say to the team, I say to them again and again, you cannot have things on your desk that look like sweets. Pencil erasers, brightly coloured thumb drives, fucking marbles even, none of this shit is okay because this fucking kid, he will eat them. He's a fucking idiot, you know? I saw him once, he ate a fucking squash ball. Stop chewing that you fucking crazy man I said, but he was not listening. Oh man, it took him like two days to finish it. Just spit it out, we have work to do, I yelled, but the kid wasn't fucking listening. That's the problem, okay?

This other time, right, he come into my office and he's got a fucking squirrel in a bag. Don't bring that fucking squirrel in a bag into my office, I shout. We have fucking strategy to discuss here and it's going to chew my stuff and get squirrel shit everywhere and, oh my God, then the fucking squirrel gets loose and the whole strategy meeting has to stop because this fucking thing is running around the room like a crazy fucking missile. And I say to the kid, why did you bring this fucking thing into my team but he cannot answer, and you know why he cannot answer? He is eating a fucking lightbulb because he thought it was a see-through lollipop. Euchhh, this kid is a pain in the hole of my ass.

Listen, you know what I'm saying here, the guy is a fucking liability, right? I can't have this guy in the factory too much for my own sanity, because of all the fucking phone calls. "Oh Mr Steiner, it's reception, Mr Grosjean has fallen off the mezzanine level again". "Hello Mr Steiner, it's reception, Mr Grosjean is here and he seems to have a very large number of cats with him", "Sorry to bother you Mr Steiner but one of your drivers is here and he seems to have got his head stuck in the fence outside again". One of my drivers? Guess which fucking driver? The one who is a stabbing pain in my entire ass place, that's who. I can't run a team like this, okay, not with some guy who goes into the workshop and tries to get into the car head first because he "forgot" which way up you go to drive. That's my problem, you see now? Like, this is the guy who can't even remember which way around a fucking baseball cap goes. I say to him, I say the front is the bit with the fucking name on it you dumb tit, but he is still confused because then he can't remember which is the front of his fucking head. The part with your fucking face on, monkey nuts. Sheesh.

Okay right, so now you say hey, come on Steiner, you're being unfair on the kid just 'cos, I dunno, he once got his leg trapped in a revolving door and he doesn't know how stairs work. He's a good driver, you say, right? Yea, well tell that to my asshole 'cos that's where all the pain is. Listen, sometimes this kid, he's got some speed and he manages not to crash it into another fucking car 'cos he saw a helicopter or he thought someone was waving to him or some shitballs whatever. But, oh my fucking eyes, the fucking moaning is driving a fucking burning sword into my Italian asshole, you know? Wah wah, the car is not fast enough, wah wah, I don't like this engine or this chassis or the flavour of the seat. Well stop trying to eat the fucking seats, you head of a dick. Always, always, he is on at me. I want this, I want that, I saw what the other teams can do. Yea, well I saw you sit on a used paper plate that had gravy on it and it got stuck to your fucking pants and then you walked around the fucking engineering office like that until it fell off when you got your arm jammed in the 3D printer, you ass face. Urgch, you know I said to him, I said if you concentrated as much on driving as you do on moaning and bringing another fucking live goose into the factory maybe last year we would have been top of the mid-field and we weren't because fucking Renault had us by the tits and you have a shit for your brain. Argh.

Hey, look, sometimes the kid is okay. Sometimes he is only the small kind of pain in my ass. And you know, hey, it's not all bad. I mean, he's still faster than Kevin.

Oh my God, I have to go, he's just come into the office and he's actually on fire. Fucking Christmas, give me fucking strength. Wanker.

RACE 9: AUSTRIA

Date: 30 June
Location: Spielberg
Full name: Fizzy Floor Cleaner Ring
Circuit type: Austrian

Austria is Red Bull's home race as their factory is located just 950 miles away in Buckinghamshire. The people who sell tiny cylinders of heart palpitations also own the very track upon which the race takes place so, as well as the usual high speeds, low lap times and dramatic elevation changes, expect to see some spikes that pop out of the kerbs when other teams' cars drive past, and maybe an enormous boulder or two rolling down a hillside. This circuit is a favourite of Daniil Kvyat because there's a shop nearby that sells the flavour of crisps he likes, which is ready salted. In fairness, he's only bought crisps once in his life.

FIVE FACTS ABOUT AUSTRIA

1. New for fans at the Austrian GP this year is a karting experience jointly set up by outspoken Austrian legends Niki Lauda and Gerhard Berger, called The Fucking Karting Shit Place.
2. One of the most popular hobbies in Austria is telling people that you will be back.
3. Legendary Austrian driver Dieter Quester will not be attending this year's race as he's got Theirry Boutsen staying that weekend and they're going to a decking show.
4. Over one third of people in Austria live in Austria.
5. Almost two thirds do as well.

THE TEAMS: HAAS

ROMAIN GROSJEAN
Nationality: French
Number: 8
Championship position last year: 14th
Nickname: Le Petit Accident

KEVIN MAGNUSSEN
Nationality: Danish
Number: 20
Championship position last year: 9th
Nickname: Ken Magnussen

THE TEAMS: HAAS

Full name: Rich Energy Haas Blurgh This Tastes Like Sticky Mouthwash F1 Team
Car: VF-19
Engine: Ferrari
Championship position last year: 5th

Haas arrived in F1 making a lot of silly noises about winning things from the off then realised it was a lot more difficult than they thought and used a specially adapted version of one of their powerful milling machines to wind their fucking necks in. Ambitions re-calibrated, they've quietly got on with delivering solid performances to the extent that they finished fifth in last year's constructor's championship, which is all the more impressive when you remember that the teams beneath them have been around for a lot longer and some of them used to be quite good. No changes to the driver line-up for this year, which pairs bungling French gap year student Romain Grosjean with frequently unnoticeable driving teddy bear Kevin "Ken" Magnussen. Grosjean is capable of good things and then suddenly going a bit erratic again, while Magnussen has wild moments before settling into the 'seems like a nice enough guy but will never win a championship' role which he can really make his own again now Stoffel Vandoorne has gone.

FAMOUS QUOTES FROM F1 HISTORY

"It is a significant degree of disappointedness with which I observe for myself that Ayrton and Alain have once again experienced a sub-optimal vehicular contact scenario."

RON DENNIS (1990)

RACE 10: GREAT BRITAIN

Date: 14 July
Location: Silverstone
Full circuit name: The Towcesterdrome
Circuit type: Brisk

The 2019 race could be Silverstone's last after organisers invoked the contract break option to avoid Bernie Ecclestone's post-2020 clause about first born sons. F1 might have a future at Silverstone if Liberty can be bothered to negotiate with BRDC bores in flat caps, and assuming Donington doesn't come up with some counter offer involving a building site with no cash. The future could be further complicated by Brexit, especially if a noisy gang of daft racists that mistakenly believes it has a moral majority objects to sponsorship from a Spanish bank or Swiss watch maker and only wants money from a proper British business of the kind that no longer exists since they've all gone bust after Britain fucked itself up the arse all because some old people once heard somebody speaking Polish in the post office.

FIVE FACTS ABOUT GREAT BRITAIN

1. The best way for Americans to understand the make-up of Great Britain is to call the whole thing England.
2. A study found that the average British person says 'sorry' 7500 times a day and sometimes even means it.
3. British people voted the Spitfire as the icon that most makes them believe their country is still important.
4. Over 60 percent of British town names are spelt that way to confuse foreigners.
5. 2019 marks the 40th anniversary of the last time a British person complained to a waiter about the food.

A SPOOKY F1 STORY

BY ZAK BROWN

 Hey guys, thanks for stopping by. Zak B here, from the McLaren place. Now I sure don't wanna scare you guys but I gotta a strange tale that I wanna share. Don't worry, it's not the one about the little Spanish boy who moaned and sighed and moaned and sighed and then found he didn't have a drive for 2019! No, but seriously, this is one weird story I wanna share with you all today.

Okay, this story starts in 2016, a few days after I started at the old place in Woking. I'm leaving the office late one night when I'm approached by this strange old lady. She was kinda tall but sorta hunched over and she was wearing a really neatly pressed headscarf so I couldn't see her face. I noticed she had really, really clean shoes. Well anyways, the lady came up to me and she gave me a kind of old timey music box, except it was made of carbon fibre and the old lady said the mechanism was "performance optimised". I don't mind telling you folks, this episode creeped me out a little. Anyways, the hunched old lady was real insistent that I took the small music box from her so I did. I mean, it was kinda cute and hey, what's the harm?

Well, the next day I recalled that it was still in my briefcase so I took it out and placed it on the shelf in my office. No big deal, right? Also, I had bigger issues to face because that very day Jenson Button confirmed that he was quitting the team for 2017. That was a real pain in the ass! But hey, we solved that problem by promoting that other guy, I forget his name, and we were all set for '17!

Leastways, that's what I thought. You know, I said to the guys, come on, '15 and '16 were tough, but things have changed now. Uncle Zak is here to make it all better. I used to say that to people all the time in my office and they would reply, "Hey, what's that weird little music box on your shelf?" Don't you worry about that, I would reply. The point is that 2017 is going to be better for us, I guarantee it. Sure, the engine didn't fire up right first time and sure, testing was pretty much a disaster, but hey, come on, things are gonna be great, right? You know, sometimes I used to stand in my office and just look at the music box and maybe even talk to it. "We're gonna have a good season, weird music box from the mysterious old lady," I would say. "Tell me it's so, music box". And then the lid would open and a small figure of a very neatly dressed man in a suit would appear, and a little tune would play. A kind of flat, monotonous tune, actually, but I guess I grew to like it. And I would stand there and listen to the music box, and then someone would enter my office and tell me that the modifications Honda has made to the engine had actually reduced horsepower even further, and I would close the music box again and silently weep inside. If only I had known what I know now...

Anyways, the '17 season comes around and, I know this sounds kinda silly, but I took that darn music box with me to the first race. I guess I believed it would bring us luck. After all, wasn't that what the old lady said when she gave it to me? "Egress one example of a hand from your pocketry area and extend it forth towards myself in a horizontal orientation with palm in the upwards positional mode," she said in her nasal old lady voice. "For I shall place upon this surface a gift item that will bring to you a significant quantity of luck". Well lemme tell you, I believed that old lady which is why I took the music box to Australia and to all the other races at the start of that season. Well gosh darnit guys, there was no good luck at all. Actually, there was only bad luck. Double retirements, unreliability, accidents. I was as frustrated as Eric was sweaty, by which I mean very! You know, the season was almost over when it occurred to me; when we scored our first points of the season in Baku I had forgotten the music box! Suddenly it was all clear! The music box didn't bring good luck at all! The music box was CURSED!

With just three races until the end, I got rid of that darned music box right away! Its curse had given us a terrible season and left me wondering, why did the mysterious old lady say it was lucky? Was she lying to me? I thought back to her closing remarks as she disappeared into the night that evening the box was given to me. "With the human emotion of sincerity I dispense to you a platitude urging that you receive not less than all of the best," she had said. "With all sarcasm vectors in place I certainly experience a feeling of hope that your season is not one of significant terribleness," she added before laughing in a weird way where she basically just said the word 'ha' over and over. I guess we'll never know who that weird old lady was, but since I got rid of her stupid music box McLaren has been on the up!

Where is the cursed music box now, you ask? Well I was gonna throw it in the trash at the end of the US Grand Prix but then someone saw me doing that and asked if they could have it. Well I tried to warn them but they weren't listening and so, well, I guess Claire Williams still has it.

RACE 11: GERMANY

Date: 28 July
Location: Hockenheim
Full name: Hockenheimringerplatzenfahrtenzone
Circuit type: Bland

After several years of titting about with an alternating system that didn't quite work, the German Grand Prix is back at Hockenheim only a year after the last time. This is thanks in part to the intervention of Toto Wolff who got involved in negotiations, shortly after borrowing someone's clothes, boots and motorcycle. Of course, the team boss is keen to keep F1 in Germany because this is Mercedes' home race for everyone except people like Toto Wolff, who work at the factory in Northamptonshire. However, the long-term future of the race is shaky since it struggles to make money and must compete against tracks in places where governments will heavily subsidise F1 as a marketing operation for tourism, something the German authorities are unwilling to do since seven people from other countries already holidayed in Germany last year.

FIVE FACTS ABOUT GERMANY

1. It is extremely rude to ask a German person how many flannels they own.
2. Middle-aged German men did not receive the memo about the unfashionableness of the moustache.
3. There is no word in German for failing to spot a low table and then falling over it.
4. The number for the German police is no, no, no.
5. Game of Thrones is a huge hit subtitled into German. As a result, the most popular name for newborn boys in Germany last year was Title Sequence.

THE TEAMS: MCLAREN

CARLOS SAINZ JR.
Nationality: Spanish
Number: 55
Championship position last year: 10th
Nickname: Neck Beard

LANDO NORRIS
Nationality: British
Number: 4
Championship position last year: n/a
Nickname: No Beard

THE TEAMS: MCLAREN

Full name: McLaren Don't Mention Those Delicious, Delicious Smokes F1 Team
Car: MCL34
Engine: Renault
Championship position last year: 6th

It's been a torrid few years for McLaren as they've had to endure poor pace, disappointing reliability and endless sighing from Fernando Alonso. A switch to Renault power last year saw some improvement in at least one of those areas and things are definitely going to get better on the last point because Alonso and his permanent air of weary resignation won't be driving for the team, so they can finally throw away all that bloody Kimoa shit that's been cluttering up the factory. Also out of the frame this year is perpetually frightened man-in-a-cat-costume Stoffel Vandoorne which means a double vacancy at the team with the biggest lake outside their factory. Alonso's place will be taken by fellow Spaniard Carlos Sainz jr, because McLaren's team chef had got really good at making patatas bravas and it seemed a shame to waste that. Vandoorne's seat, meanwhile, will be filled by big-haired British driving child Lando Norris who is tipped for good things by sports reporters who have been furiously Googling Star Wars quotes in the hope they can shoehorn something into a headline if he wins.

ALONSO AS AMBASSADOR

After quitting as their driver at the end of last season, Fernando Alonso is to stay with McLaren as a 'Racing Ambassador'. Here is what his duties include;

- Can have a go in the new F1 car but mustn't drive it too fast to avoid upsetting team's other drivers.

- Must not get out of drive in latest F1 car shouting, "And why couldn't I have had one like that you bastards?"

- Must only reply to questions about recent years driving with the team by saying, "It was an experience" and not, for example, "It was shit".

- Allowed to keep bringing own branded caps from home.

- Can theatrically roll eyes whenever anyone mentions Honda.

RACE 12: HUNGARY

Date: 4 August
Location: Budapest
Full name: The Hungarohungarohippping
Circuit type: Low-to-middling

A stalwart of the F1 calendar, the Hungarian race has come to mark the mid-point of the season and the last twisty, bumpy push before the summer break. It's around this point that we should have a good idea of whether Ferrari are still full of optimism and have yet to piss it all away, or are already slightly dejected and having a mild tantrum in which they claim they didn't want to be stupid champions anyway. The Budapest track sometimes gives us memorable moments, like the time in 2015 when Johnny Herbert bought some new after shave from a stall outside the circuit and spent the rest of the weekend being attacked by a crow.

FIVE FACTS ABOUT HUNGARY

1. The national dish of Hungary is to eat your own hand.
2. Tourism in Hungary's capital took a severe hit last year after someone stole the airport.
3. Seven out of ten Hungarians refuse to take part in surveys.
4. Hungary once told everyone they were the first country to land on the moon because they didn't think anyone would check.
5. If you are on holiday in Hungary and someone offers you a 'pohárszék' do not accept as this means 'sideboard' and you will never get it on the plane.

I'M SO GLAD I'M NOT IN F1 ANYMORE

BY NICO ROSBERG

Hi guys! Nico here! Nico Rosberg! You know, the 2016 Formula 1 World Champion? That's right! Nico Rosberg! Hi! You can't see this but I'm doing that thing where I come right up to the camera and actually touch the lens with one finger! I hope I don't get told off by the camera guy for getting race grease on the glass again!

For sure, people often ask me, don't you miss the excitement of Formula 1? And I say, hey, you know what's better than the excitement of Formula 1? The excitement of being able to make plans on a Sunday! Trust me, it's a heck of a rush when you can say, sure I can come to your barbecue this weekend instead of 'oh I'm so sorry I can't make the barbecue, I have to go drive in a Formula 1 race in, like, Japan or something'! I sure don't miss that one, I can tell you guys!

For sure, people just don't realise how time consuming being a Formula 1 driver was. Come on guys, it's not just weekends you know! Wheesh! It's exhausting! There's not a day goes by when I don't think, thank goodness I'm not having to do all that testing and simulator work and strategy and I can just sit here watching Homes Under The Hammer in my pyjamas. I bet all the guys on the F1 for 2019 wish they could do that too! But they can't, because they are F1 drivers.

For sure, sometimes people ask me if I miss the speed and the adrenaline of Formula 1 racing and I say, no way guys, are you crazy? You can get adrenaline in other ways you know! For example, last week I drove to Nice to buy some adhesive sealing strips to eliminate a slight draught coming through a window frame in our spare bedroom. Did I call ahead to the store or check stock levels online first? No! I took a chance, and that chance paid off because actually they had plenty of the correct adhesive sealing strips in stock! Phew! But that drive there, when I realised I was heading into the unknown, it was quite a rush, I tell you.

For sure, people ask if I miss the glamour of the Formula 1 races and yes, for sure, sometimes that was pretty cool. But hey, I can still go to F1 races if I want to. After all, I was only Formula 1 World Champion of F1 three years ago, in 2016, and so I'm still a well-known face in the paddock. "Hey Nico!" people say wherever I go. "You're back again! Weren't you just at the last race, and the one before that?" So yea, I can still do that, I hope. That's enough glamour for me, thank you guys! I don't need to actually drive the cars, unless they asked me to which of course they could but I guess they haven't thought to do that yet and maybe they should, right! Ha ha ha ha ha! Ha! But hey, I don't need that for the glamour any more than I need to, I don't know, go to Paris Fashion Week and hang around with some cool people going, "Hey, I'm Lewis Hamilton, look at my strange jacket!" like a total loser or something!

For sure, people ask me if I would be interested in winning more than one drivers' championship and I always say, come on guys, one is enough. You don't eat more than one croissant or have more than one cup of coffee in the morning do you? You don't own more than one car? Oh wait, actually I do. Bad example. Look, my point is that one F1 championship is enough and you'd have to be an absolute idiot to try for two or six or whatever.

For sure guys, what I'm saying here is that I totally don't miss Formula 1 and I'm totally busy with my life so there is no way I would go back unless they asked me! Can the current F1 guys go get a cappuccino at 11am in a pair of shorts and then just sit by the harbour weeping? I think not! Right?

Okay, that's it guys, that's all from me, Nico. Nico Rosberg. I was the 2016 Formula 1 World Champion.

RACE 13: BELGIUM

Date: 1 September
Location: Spa-Francorchamps
Full name: Le Thierry Boutsenodrome
Circuit type: Woody

F1 returns from the summer break to a classic track that's probably enough to lure back fans who might have been thinking of knocking it on the head for this season if it's been really boring. Spa brings exciting speed, giddy elevation changes and the chance to have a chocolate pancake for breakfast without being told off by your mum. The main benefit of Spa, however, is the chance for commentators and pundits to go on endlessly about 'changeable weather' and 'the fickle Ardennes climate' as if coming to Belgium suddenly makes all of them Michael fucking Fish.

FIVE FACTS ABOUT BELGIUM

1. Local legend Thierry Boutsen will be unable to attend this year's race as he's having some decking delivered.
2. Contrary to the old joke there are in fact lots of famous Belgians such as Jason Stathaam, Bruno Maars, and Jean-Luc Bono out of U2.
3. Belgians are famous for drinking strong beer and eating rich chocolate and thick, doughy waffles but there are other pastimes popular amongst people here such as struggling to breath and spending a long, long time in the bathroom.
4. The most popular sport in Belgium is humming.
5. Belgian bank notes carry the motto 'switch to landscape mode' after the country's constitution was mixed up with the instruction manual for a printer.

THE TEAMS: RACING POINT

SERGIO PEREZ
Nationality: Mexican
Number: 11
Championship position last year: 8th
Nickname: Checo

LANCE STROLL
Nationality: Canadian
Number: 18
Championship position last year: 18th
Nickname: Checo Book

THE TEAMS: RACING POINT

Full name: SportPesa Racing Point Don't Mention Force India F1 Team
Car: RP19
Engine: Mercedes
Championship position last year: 7th

One time de facto midfield champions (assuming what was once called 'The Sauber Situation'), the team formerly known as Force India began to suffer once Vijay Mallya decided to lose all of his money while slowly transforming into a deflating wizard. Their position seemed particularly perilous during the 2018 season until, happily, Lance Stroll told his daddy that he wanted a racing team for his birthday. After that things started to look up, apart from the looming prospect of having to give Lance Stroll a drive. They even came seventh in the constructors' title despite having to throw all their points in the bin during the summer break and now they're back for the 2019 season with a new name that still doesn't sound right, like a fake team made up for a movie about F1. Forcing Pindia retain strong Mercedes power and a proven track record of making quick cars, along with solid performer Sergio Perez in the car that will have to do all the points scoring. Perez has some history of crash 'n' bash, not least with his own team mate, but there's much less risk of that happening this season, at least until he comes up to lap him.

FAMOUS QUOTES
FROM F1 HISTORY

"You know, Formula 1 is like, is speed but also all is pretty girl and also helicopter and boat and bouncy bouncy have nice time, smell like hair, is sexy you know? Mmm."

FLAVIO BRIATORE (2005)

RACE 14: ITALY

Date: 8 September
Location: Monza
Full name: Autodromo Nazionale di Ferrari 348 e Land Rover Discovery Mark Uno
Circuit type: Presto

Nothing gets an F1 fan over-enunciating foreign words like a pretentious man in an Italian restaurant quite as much as Monza with its evocative corner names like Parabolica, Grande and Marea 20v. The Italian race is always short and intense, sort of like the espresso of Grand Prix, except it doesn't make your hands all clammy for an hour afterwards. As you'd expect, support for the home team is powerful and the crowd at Monza is always a sea of red shirts, which was terribly unfortunate during the 2014 race when someone accidentally released a bull into the grandstands. The bull later slunk away in despair after getting sick of people in €90 baseball caps whinging about how unfair it was that Ferrari weren't being allowed to win the championship.

FIVE FACTS ABOUT ITALY

1. Some Italians want a UK-style exit from the EU saying they are tired of pretending to obey their rules.
2. The most popular hobby in Italy is having an extremely angry telephone conversation in a narrow alleyway.
3. The fastest car ever made in Italy is a dented 2004 Fiat Punto driven by a smoking man in sunglasses.
4. Italian law textbooks are filed in the fiction section.
5. The top rated TV shows in Italy are Nude X Factor, Strictly Come Naked Dancing and Come Dine Without Any Clothes On.

THE 2019 TITLE FIGHT

F1 journalist TRENTHAM SLEAVES gives his view on who will win this season's drivers' championship

There's always a frisson of excitement at the start of a new Formula 1 season. The unearthing of the trusty passport. The confirming of the reservation at the delightful hotel in which one will be staying. The packing of the faithful *sac de voyage*. It's all so familiar and yet so new. As I once said to my old mate Anthony Davidson as we sat together on a flight, *"Plus ca change, plus c'est la même F1"*. I'll never forget his reply which was "Please stop talking to me or I'll ask to move seats"! Good old Ant, such a marvellous sense of humour!

As we move towards the front door, gathering up the pass that will get us into each and every race for free, and we head towards the first of many flights that will whisk us to a front row seat for all the action once more, we must ask the question that will be burning on the lips of everyone from important people like drivers, team bosses and journalists, right down to the ordinary punters. The question is simply this; who will win this year's Formula 1 drivers' world championship?

As I sit here at my 15-inch Macbook Pro in my beautiful kitchen at home, I struggle to think of a year when the title fight has seemed so hard to call before the season's commencement, aside from perhaps last year and the one before that, and the years prior to that. Testing teaches us so much and yet so little and that is what makes it so fascinating, especially for those of us who were just in Barcelona to see it. I remember once remarking to dear old Nigel Mansell that trying to predict an F1 champion pre-season is like trying to predict which leaf will fall first from the many trees in my garden, to which he replied, "This is a private party, leave immediately"! I don't know why some say 'Our Nige' has no sense of humour when I have always found him quite the wit!

To the runners and riders in this year's Formula 1 season then and one has to start with good old Lewis Hamilton, the reigning king and an early favourite for glory in claiming 2019's *grandest* of *prix*. Some have found Lew to be a tricky fish but I have always found, on the many occasions we have chatted, that if you are direct with him then he will return the courtesy, even if just to unleash one of his customary 'cool' sayings such as "Just leave me alone, man". Will the lad from Stevenage clinch a sixth title this year? It's certainly possible!

Mr Hamilton's plan could be spoilt, however, by the resurgent Ferrari team and a certain Herr Vettel who is as steely and determined on the track as he is cheeky and playful off it. It cannot be understated how much dear Seb loves pranks, such as the time he impishly had me banned from all Ferrari property in the paddock for the remainder of the season! Such a jester! To be serious, though, will the German ace finally score that fifth WC? You would have to say that he might!

Discount not, however, Seb's new *fratello d'armi* in the form of the ever-talented Charlie Leclerc who is fast, fearless and, it must be said, very funny. "Your command of French is terrible!" he once quipped to me at an exclusive event during the Bahrain Grand Prix weekend and he did so in English, which was an irony I'm sure was not lost on him as he walked away to talk to someone else! Could Monsieur L. *voler le championship de pilotes* from under the *nez* of his more experienced team mate? As they say in France, *c'est possible!*

Yet foolish would be the man who would dismiss those rampant Red Bulls at this stage, and in particular the youthful exuberance of young Max Verstappen. This fearless Dutch warrior kowtows to no one on track and I'm sure there are plenty of F1's wiser heads who he has told to "piss off" just as he did to me! Without question, young Stappo is maturing nicely without losing any of his edge but does that mean he could be in line to cause a stir with his first driving title? I would not wager against it!

As for the rest of the pack, bet not against the firm focus of Valtteri Bottas in a rampant Three-Pointed Star nor upsets from the young blades in Renaults, Racing Points and the occasional Haas. Furthermore, how could one forget the newly elevated Pierre Gasly? In some ways this French flyer reminds me of his countryman, *Le Profeseur* himself, my old mate Al Prost, although it remains to be seen whether he will be truly mimic Prost in his speed, his success and his hilarious jape of having me literally thrown off a boat into Monaco harbour! All I would say is, *ne pas* count against him!

Who, then, will take the ultimate prize in the 2019 Formula World Championship? As I said earlier, it's a tough one to call but I'm going to stick my neck out right here and now as I write prior to my luxury flight to Australia and say, quite honestly, it could be anyone. The most important thing is, whatever the outcome, I will be at every race with a prime seat to witness all of the action because it's always worth bearing in mind, whenever and wherever the race, I will be there and you won't!

RACE 15: SINGAPORE

Date: 22 September
Location: Marina Bay
Full name: The Road Closed Circuit
Circuit type: Dark

The race that fans of medium speed corners and floodlighting have been waiting for, Singapore is the drivers' chance to crack out those clear visors that always look wrong somehow. The now-familiar track is made useable in nocturnal conditions by over three million watts of lighting power giving a level of brightness in excess of that found in a football stadium and almost as much as in the kitchen of a cheap rented flat. Celebrities are usually thin on the ground in this race, giving a welcome break to the people who do the live captions for TV grid walks, but it's thought Nelson Piquet jr. might be in town for the weekend, if he can find somewhere to crash.

FIVE FACTS ABOUT SINGAPORE

1. Singapore banned chewing gum in 2004, along with sunglasses and smoking, moves that were branded 'racist' by the Association Of Cool People.
2. The name Singapore derives from 'lion city'. Residents of modern day Singapore still haven't found these lions and are permanently on edge as a result.
3. Singapore is the only city in the world that is entirely wipe clean.
4. The decision to make the Singapore GP a night race came from Bernie Ecclestone, to the delight of local electricity supplier Elecclestone Limited.
5. The national pastime of Singapore is sitting quietly reading a book about business unless told otherwise.

THE TEAMS: ALFA ROMEO

KIMI RAIKKONEN
Nationality: Whatever
Number: Yea, you know, it's gnnnnrr, phnurk
Championship position last year: Sure, it's, I dunno.
Nickname: Yea, Whatever, I Don't Know, Put What You
Like, Sure

ANTONIO GIOVINAZZI
Nationality: Italian
Number: 99
Championship position last year: n/a
Nickname: Tony Nasty

THE TEAMS: ALFA ROMEO

Full name: Alfa Romeo Definitely Not Sauber Racing
Car: C38
Engine: Ferrari
Championship position last year: 8th

The artist formerly known as Sauber is now fully Alfa Romeo, with retired founder Peter Sauber changing his name to Peter Alfa Romeo just to keep things consistent. The move makes sense as nothing will help to market Alfa Romeo road cars like a Swiss racing team that isn't very good any more. Big news this year, aside from the name change, is the arrival of ageing not-giving-a-shit enthusiast Kimi Raikkonen who briefly noticed that his overalls had changed colour at pre-season testing and will probably twig he's now at a different team at some point. Raikkonen is still capable of pulling an impressive result out of the bag if he can bothered which, in fairness, he usually can't. The mumbling Finn is joined at Sauber Romeo by Ferrari Driver Academy protégé Antonio Giovinazzi who has been skirting around the edges of F1 for a while, mainly because he was a sort of free gift that got included automatically in your order if you bought Ferrari engines.

COMING UP ON SKY F1

For F1 fans in the UK, 2019 sees Channel 4 move to highlights-only coverage, save for the British Grand Prix. If you've got Sky, however, there's a whole channel of F1 stuff and hours of airtime that needs filling in the run-up to a race. Here are some of the exciting VT packages to look forward to this year.

- Karun Chandhok spends lunchtime with George Russell to see what a rookie F1 driver would order in Wagamama.

- Natalie Pinkham joins Lando Norris in the Bristol Airport branch of WH Smith to learn more about how he would buy a birthday card for an elderly relative.

- Johnny Herbert goes to the cinema in Stockport with Daniel Ricciardo to see if the move to Renault has given him a new approach to dealing with a bunch of teenagers who won't stop fucking talking during a film.

- Damon Hill accompanies Robert Kubica on a trip back to Poland, during which he repeatedly calls him 'Robin' to see how the comeback king copes with someone who keeps getting his name wrong in a social situation.

- Martin Brundle breaks into Alexander Albon's apartment at 3am to see how the newcomer handles being woken by a gang of masked men smashing up his furniture and shouting "WHERE IS IT?" without being more specific.

RACE 16: RUSSIA

Date: 29 September
Location: Sochi
Full name: The Rolex Rolex Rolex Circuit Of Light Industrial Estate
Circuit type: Tedious

Everyone's favourite extremely long procession around a grey zone of medium sized businesses and redundant athletes' sex pods returns for another joyless year. Russia is the ideal race for anyone struggling to remember how 'Rolex' is spelt and people who enjoy seeing the end-of-race proceedings infiltrated by a rat-faced man who wants to hurt people who displease him. Not Adrian Sutil, the other one. At this year's race the crowd will once again be given the chance to root for local boy Daniil Kvyat, unless instructed otherwise for strategic reasons.

FIVE FACTS ABOUT RUSSIA

1. Russia has proven itself expert at infiltrating the discourse of other countries.
2. Russia is excellent.
3. I live in Wisconsin, USA and Mr Donald Trump is a very great man.
4. Vladimir Putin, most handsome president of Russia, is a sexual man of all.
5. Please send help we work for no money help help help Podgornaja 83, Murmansk, Ru…

2019 LINE UP CHANGES

WITH CRAZY DAVE COULTHARD

Och aye tha noo muthafuckas! Crazy Dave Coulthard comin' atcha all season long wit' ma bulging package of highlights. 'Cept tha GB GP when you get ma full length, know wha''am sayin'? Freeizzle to airizzle.

So tha zero-nineteen Fiddy Wizzle season is shapin' up to be hotter than Crazy D's legs in a high humiditizzle environment wit' these super tight trousaz. Compromised breathabilitee. But you cats might be wonderin' wha'appnin' wit' ma so solid brothaz on tha drivin' crew cuz, unlike Crazy D's testez in these jeanz, there been a lot of movement.

Okay, let's take it from tha top. First of all, ma brotha from a drunker motha, K Raikk, he move from tha Fo'rrari to tha Saub-daddy, 'cept it ain't call that no mo' cuz dem be re-named by dem espresso shot snake logo muthafunkers Alfo' Romeo. Will dis affect Da Raikkmeister? Nope, dat cat don't care. I was takizzle a shizzle. Fo' sho'.

So Da Raikk's mic at tha Prancizzle Ho' be taken by ma Frenchie muthalover CLC, and dat homie got tha skillz to pay tha billaz. Hot damn. Don't be comin' to Crazy D all surprised when that young brotha be steppin' to Sebby V with tha superior qualifying or finish posizzle. Impressizzle car controzzle. Dang.

Since we chattin' 'bout people what is good at tha drivin', my so smiley homedog D Ricci gone binned tha

Itty Bitty Bull and now dat cat in da Reno', yo. Improvizzle mid-fieizzled resultizzles. Dat mean Ricci's place at tha RB be taken by tha boy P Gas, an' he gonna have to find some mad flavas to keep up wit' ma homebreadren Maximum V cuz that homeboy be makin' moves like Crazy D in a club, know wha'am sayin'? Nicelee maturizzle abilitizzles. Hoopla!

Shizzle be gettin' real at tha crew what used to be Fo' Cindia, but now is tha Racin' P. Big daddy Lawry be laying out tha Canadian benjamins and that mean a drivin' seat for ma big browed, small talent brotha, Lanny St Roll. Mmm, dat be some mighty fine nepotizzle.

Ma homies at MC Laren, they got a new vibe since Nando got sick of they shizzle and now ma rally dad homie Carlo to tha Zee be on tha scene, 'long wit' ma ain't-even-shavin'-yet brotha LaNo. Is they gonna be scorin' like Tha D back in tha day at a grid girl convention? Hey, it can't get much more shizzle than a coupla years ago-izzle. Boom!

Over at tha TR, also known as ReBu2, ma spotty faced Soviet homie Dee Kay be back like a cat, and he be alongside Thai bride academy child Al Albon, fo' sho'. Also-izzle, I fo'got to tell y'all that K Raikk at tha Romeo be joined by ma adequate breadren Ant Giovinazzizzleizzle. Well some homie gotta drive tha ting, you get me, yea?

Lastly, tings ain't been gravy fo' ma brothas from anotha motha in Oxfordshizzle, Will.i.ams. But hey, they got rid of tha '18-spec fuckwizzles and in come a stone cold solid, the owl-face broken hand homie that be Robbie Koobeekay, and he be playin' 'longside heard-good-tings pre-pubes brotha G Russ. Dem cats sure can get tha crowd jumpin' on tha wheels of magnees so they jus' gotta hope tha new car ain't total dog shizzle, 'pecially now they lost ma homie P Lo.

What can I say, homedogs. It's been emotionizzle. Dis season gonna be bitchin' wit' all tha on-track action and shiz. You cats ain't gonna be able to sit down. Which is just tha same as Crazy D in these trousaz. Yow!

RACE 17: JAPAN

Date: 13 October
Location: Suzuka
Full name: The Hondadrome
Circuit type: Eight-y

F1 stays at Suzuka for 2019, which is great news because it's an excellent track and all the fans are here anyway since they just stay quietly in their seats until the next race. The track is rightly famed for legendary corners like Spoon, so-called because it looks like a teaspoon. Other corners include Middle Finger, Upsidedown Shark and the fearsome Loch Ness Monster Or, Oh I Dunno, Maybe A Petrol Pump Or Something? Many world titles have been won in Japan, but that's because it was once at the end of the season, not crammed in as part of what seems to be a schedule created to study the effects of severe jetlag.

FIVE FACTS ABOUT JAPAN

1. Audibly coughing in Japan incurs such embarrassment that you must move to another city.
2. Japan's top-rated TV show is No Thank You! in which unsuspecting contestants are invited to a job interview then attacked with hammers by a man dressed as a cat.
3. People in the west imagine Japan to be very high-tech yet some old traditions remain, such as having a turtle in your bed for reasons that don't easily translate.
4. The Japanese flag is supposed to have more details on it but they got rubbed off.
5. On 29 June 1978 a train on the Tokyo to Yokohama line ran two minutes late due to a bad duck. As a result of this unacceptable situation, all of Japan had to be scrapped and started again.

DANIIL KVYAT
Nationality: Russian
Number: 26
Championship position last year: n/a
Nickname: Ol' Two Is

ALEXANDER ALBON
Nationality: Thai
Number: 23
Championship position last year: n/a
Nickname: 'Damon'

THE TEAMS: TORO ROSSO

Full name: Red Bull Second Division Toro Rosso Honda
Car: STR14
Engine: Honda
Championship position last year: 9th

The 'spare' Red Bull team had a typically wank time of it last year, creaking in at ninth in the constructors' championship while failing to beat teams with less money and the one that had all its points taken away half way through. However, Toro Rosso has never been about finishing in the top half of the table, which is good because they never do. Instead, their job in F1 is two-fold. First of all, they're on the grid to advertise some new kind of revolting soft drink spin-off that tastes like the stuff they use to clean nuclear waste off boat hulls. Secondly, they're the nursery for new driver talent that might one day get to drive a truly decent car. On that note, things haven't gone entirely plan for 2019 because one of their drivers is Daniil Kvyat who passed through this process, got promoted to Red Bull, made a cock of it, dropped back down to Toro Rosso and was binned off, only to be re-hired for this season like someone desperately calling their ex-girlfriend to see if she'll be their date to a wedding. Meanwhile, the other driver is Alexander Albon, who was on the Red Bull Junior Team only to get ditched and then re-hired, which suggests the biggest product of the young driver programme is awkward phone calls. Albon will be the first Thai driver in Formula 1 for over 60 years, as he was born in the beautiful city of London, Thailand and went to school in Ipswich. Presumably the one in Thailand.

FAMOUS QUOTES FROM F1 HISTORY

"Hold on lads, I think I've got a plan..."

ROSS BRAWN (2009)

RACE 18: MEXICO

Date: 27 October
Location: Mexico City
Full name: Circuito de Unusualamente Located Seating
Circuit type: Stadiumy

This year the Mexican Grand Prix is flipped with the US race in the schedule, perhaps to put a pointless, ineffective wall invented by a doll-handed moron between the two events. This GP can sometimes deliver excitement and having the track run through a baseball stadium remains a delightfully unusual touch, especially as this year the race clashes with an actual baseball game which organisers are refusing to cancel.

FIVE FACTS ABOUT MEXICO

1. One of the biggest public holidays in Mexico is *el festival de clasificación de esa olla de monedas de baja denominación en tu dormitorio* or the festival of sorting out that little pot of low denomination coins in your bedroom.
2. The national sport of Mexico is shouting 'Hey! You!" to someone across a patch of open ground.
3. Contrary to popular belief, no one in Mexico has seen your house keys. Where did you last have them?
4. The Escort Mexico was named after the 1970 London to Mexico World Cup Rally, a needlessly difficult event set up by accident after organisers didn't realise the blue bit on a world map usually means sea.
5. The drink of Mexico is tequila, which is why national holidays are immediately followed by another, quieter national holiday.

F1 X THE CHEMICAL BROTHERS

Just before the start of the season F1 announced a collaboration with top musical beat duo The Chemical Brothers based around a 15,000bpm remix labelled NEEEUM. The Brothers agreed to speak exclusively to Sniff Petrol.

SP: So, tell us how this collaboration came about.

Terry Chemical
We were working on our new album when we got the call from F1.

Kenny Chemical
And I was like, wow, F1. Some of their stuff is really great.

Terry Chemical
And then you realised you were getting mixed up.

Kenny Chemical
Yea, I was thinking of U2.

Terry Chemical
But F1 is pretty cool so we said yea, let's talk. And they said, we're looking for something to make Formula 1 more youthful and cool and cutting edge.

Kenny Chemical
And we said that sounds perfect since we're two middle aged blokes who've been doing this since the mid-nineties.

Terry Chemical

Well yeah, they didn't want it to be *too* cutting edge. So we said this seemed like something we could do.

Kenny Chemical

But I said whatever we did, it had to have a dog in a crash helmet.

Terry Chemical

Don't start this again Ken.

Kenny Chemical

I mean, that was a deal breaker for me. Will there be a dog in a crash helmet? No dog in a crash helmet, no deal.

Terry Chemical

Fortunately they said sure, do whatever you want.

Kenny Chemical

And then I said, what about a dog in a crash helmet... in space.

Terry Chemical

We later found out that at this point they tried calling Fatboy Slim but he was busy.

Kenny Chemical

And the F1 guys, they said 'oh, but we don't do F1 races in space' and I said, well there you are then, perhaps you should. Perhaps you should do Formula 1 races in space with dogs in crash helmets then, eh?

Terry Chemical
They got a bit funny at this point and, to be honest, our agent was pretty pissed off.

Ian Chemical (agent)
I was actually.

Kenny Chemical
Shut up Ian.

Terry Chemical
Yeah, we only clung on to the gig because Urban Cookie Collective said no and by then it was too late to find anyone else.

Ian Chemical
You know what I call Fatboy Slim? FART boy Slim. Ha ha ha haaaar!

SP: Sorry but are either of you actually in The Chemical Brothers?

Terry Chemical
Ummmm… no.

Ian Chemical (agent)
Our real surname is Carmichael if that helps.

Kenny Chemical
Shut up Ian you tit. DOGS IN SPACE.

RACE 19: UNITED STATES

Date: 3 November
Location: Austin
Full name: Circuit of the Gosh Darn Bigly Greatest
United States of God Bless America
Circuit type: Hilly

Formula 1 once again rolls into the famously laid back and outward looking southern city of Austin to great excitement within the place and absolute disinterest, verging on suspicions of socialism, outside of the city limits. This year the US race happens the week after the Mexican Grand Prix so expect all the teams and media to arrive wearing some terrible 'traditional' clothing that they will immediately regret buying and never wear again.

FIVE FACTS ABOUT THE USA

1. The bedrocks of American life are freedom of speech and the right to get gunned down in a shopping mall.
2. The last state to enter the union was Hawaii, a momentous event that led directly to the making of Magnum P.I.
3. When Americans talk about their 'five a day' they mean blocks of cheese.
4. Americans were asked what they'd like to see on the next generation of bank notes, as a result of which the new $10 bill will depict 'hotter chicks'.
5. Austin Texas was also the name of the hero in Johnny Herbert's ill-fated detective novels.

THE TEAMS: WILLIAMS

ROBERT KUBICA
Nationality: Polish
Number: 88
Championship position last year: n/a
Nickname: The Owl

GEORGE RUSSELL
Nationality: British
Number: 63
Championship position last year: n/a
Nickname: Oh look, it's George Russell

THE TEAMS: WILLIAMS

Full name: ROKiT Sorry The Shift Key's Playing Up
Williams Racing
Car: FW42
Engine: Mercedes
Championship position last year: 10th

Painfully located at the arse end of everything, it's former world champions Williams. For several recent seasons McLaren thought they'd got it sealed up as the most heartbreakingly shite former championship winning team until this lot came along and said, 'Hold my Martini'. Except they can't even do that any more because the stripy booze has buggered off leaving the team with a horrible graduated fade on their livery and a typographically challenged sponsor that no one has heard of. As is generally the way with once great teams, senior personnel talked a confident game about the new season just before testing went disastrously, like heavily branded versions of the Iraqi information minister. Continuing the dictatorship theme, they then killed off the one bloke who seemed quite reasonable. On the plus side, things can't get worse for Williams because they don't have Lance Stroll driving for them anymore. Instead, bird-faced old timer Robert Kubica makes his post-rebuild comeback alongside Lego hair Mercedes baby George Russell who is sure to give it his all, as long as it doesn't clash with his GCSEs.

FOR SALE

F1 memorabilia (various), including…

- Motorsport-grade Martini glasses
- F1-spec headphones (labelled P. Lowe)
- How To Drive An F1 Car book (labelled L. Stroll)
- Russian shit

WANTED

- Hope

Call Grove 4562, ask for Claire

RACE 20: BRAZIL

Date: 17 November
Location: Sao Paulo
Full name: Circuito de Ayrton Senna e The Legendary Ayrton Senna
Circuit type: Legendary

As the season nears its end, the action moves to that place that always seemed like a good way to end things but, disappointingly, isn't where it stops anymore. Nonetheless, something usually happens on the Sao Paulo track, even if it's just an ever-growing stream of liquid effluent on the track. Or, as we used to call it, Pastor Maldonado.

FIVE FACTS ABOUT BRAZIL

1. Brazil is the traditional home of someone doing a jiggly arse dance in a costume that makes them look a bit like a peacock on a Brazilian GP opening montage.
2. Brazil is the world centre of Fiats you don't quite recognise.
3. The racing driver Ayrton Senna was Brazilian, although no one ever really mentions this.
4. Damon Hill rarely enjoys his time in Brazil as his name sounds a lot like the Portuguese for 'self-tapping screws'.
5. Brazil's biggest exports are iron ore, oil, racing drivers and people related to those racing drivers who also want to have a racing career.

ST. WILLIAM'S SCHOOL FOR GIRLS
Oxford 7224

Friday 8th March 2019

Dear Sir Frank,

I'm writing about your daughter, Claire, and her current situation here at St. William's School for Girls.

I must start by saying that, by and large, Claire is an exemplary pupil. She has been a superb head girl and she was an absolute rock in running the recent cake sale which, as you may have seen in the school newsletter, raised over £60 for underprivileged horses.

The reason I am writing to you is to share my concerns about Claire's running of the school Formula 1 team. It goes without saying that we're extremely proud of our motorsport activities here at St. William's and the whole school has really got behind recent efforts such as the work of young Susie Wolff in Year 11 and her marvellous Formula E project. You may also recall a girl from a few years above Claire called Monisha who ran things in F1 with some pretty solid results, at least until she let that van der Garde boy into the school grounds and couldn't get him to leave.

Against this background of motorsport achievement, it pains me to note that under Claire's watch the Formula 1 team is not doing well. A less charitable verdict might be that it is actually something of a disaster. I was particularly disheartened and not a little disappointed to discover that for the recent school outing to Barcelona, Claire had not completed her coursework in time.

This is not the only piece of recent bad news. As you might be aware, Claire has been receiving help with running the school team from a delightful young boy called Patrick Lowe who attends St. Bernie's Boys' School. With some shock, I learnt this week that he and Claire have had some kind of falling out and he will no longer be able to assist with team chores.

I must confess I am also rather troubled that in future Claire will not receive a little financial help in running the school team from the Martini family in the village who are known and liked by all of us. Instead, she seems to have accepted a donation from an organisation called 'Rokit' which is frankly a mystery to me and seems to be the kind of fly-by-night business one would not want associated with the good name of this institution.

You know Claire better than I and you will no doubt be aware of what a good natured and upbeat young lady she is, but I cannot help feeling that when it comes to the school motor racing team she is putting on a brave face and, in truth, does not enjoy the task at all. Furthermore, it gives me no pleasure whatsoever to say that I fear she is not very good at it.

Here at St. Jackie's we always encourage our girls to stand on their own two feet and to play fair, but on this occasion and with regard to your daughter and the school F1 team I am prepared to bend the rules when I say, Sir Frank, would you be able to help Claire with her homework?

Yours sincerely,

Elizabeth Blanchard
Head teacher

RACE 21: ABU DHABI

Date: 1 December
Location: Yas Marina
Full name: The Light Up Hotel Snor-o-drome
Circuit type: Straddled

For the first time since 1963 the Formula 1 season tips into December even though it started a bit early and perhaps, you know, maybe there are too many races or something. The action comes to a climax, or perhaps just a running dribble into some dust, here at the circuit that's known for the excitement of wondering when it will go dark... oh wait, there it is. Look, they've put the lights on.

FIVE FACTS ABOUT ABU DHABI

1. Abu Dhabi is the largest of the United Arab Emirates and, by a narrow margin, the tidiest.
2. The origins of the name Abu Dhabi are uncertain, but scholars think it might have been one of the characters in the background of the Star Wars canteen.
3. Like many places in the Middle East, Abu Dhabi has a thriving ex-pat community of terrible twats.
4. Before oil was found, Abu Dhabi was known for the pearl trade, hence its nickname, 'The Sweaty Apple'.
5. There are only four interesting facts about Abu Dhabi.

FAMOUS QUOTES FROM F1 HISTORY

"Oh my saints, thank God that's over."

LUCA BADOER (2009)

THANKS
Ted Kravitz
Ben Lucareli
J, D & M

Printed in Great Britain
by Amazon